For Cindy and Fadi.
How could I have done it without you?
Thank you for taking care of me.
Eternally grateful.

Pigeonhole Books creates children's
picture books for blended, divorced,
multicultural and same-sex families.
It is a gentle resource that aims to deal
with life's challenges through beautiful
illustrations and loving words.

ISBN: 978-0-9925382-0-0

www.pigeonholebooks.com

A.S. Chung

A BRAND NEW DAY

A Banana Split Story

Illustrations by Paula Bossio

PIGEONHOLE
BOOKS

I love Mondays and Tuesdays when I get to stay with my Dad,

I get to help make dinner with recipes from his notepad.

I am good at chopping tomatoes, eating them along the way,
I really enjoy cooking and could do it almost every day.

I love Wednesdays and Thursdays when I'm with my Mum,
I get to help in the garden and be a green thumb.

I am great at pulling out the yucky, stubborn weeds,

I can tell the difference between all types of seeds.

I love Fridays and Saturdays when I'm with my father,

I can read my books or paint whichever I would rather?

I ask him which one he would prefer to do,

I get excited when he says, "let's do two!"

I love lazy Sundays when I return to mother,

I spend the whole day playing with my cute step brother.

I have hot chocolate and biscuits for tea,

I give him some too and he giggles with glee!

I love the breezy, sun-kissed school break in the spring,

I spend it with mum and we do almost everything.

I smile and giggle when we play hide and seek,
I never tell Mum when I take a sneak peek.

I love the summer months when it's really hot,
I go camping with Daddy, raining or not.

I walk our cute puppy and play in the sun,
I laugh in delight from having so much fun.

I love every single day of the week,

I get cuddles and kisses on my cheek.

I love both my parents as much as they love me,

I know we're apart but we will always be three.

CPSIA information can be obtained
at www.ICGtesting.com
Printed in the USA
LVHW072344170423
744621LV00001B/4

* 9 7 8 0 9 9 2 5 3 8 2 0 0 *